Otherwise Engaged

Other books by Simon Gray

PLAYS

Butley
The Idiot
Spoiled
Dutch Uncle
Wise Child
Sleeping Dog

NOVELS

Colmain
Little Portia
Simple People
A Comeback for Stark
 (*published under the pseudonym Hamish Reade*)

Simon Gray

OTHERWISE ENGAGED

A Richard Seaver Book
The Viking Press   *New York*

For Harold
Two summers 1971 and 1975

Otherwise Engaged

OTHERWISE ENGAGED was first presented on 30th July 1975, at the Queen's Theatre by Michael Codron with the following cast:

SIMON	Alan Bates
DAVE	Ian Charleson
STEPHEN	Nigel Hawthorne
JEFF	Julian Glover
DAVINA	Jacqueline Pearce
WOOD	Benjamin Whitrow
BETH	Mary Miller

Directed by Harold Pinter

Act One

The living-room of the HENCH's *house in London. It is both elegant and comfortable, but not large. Two sofas, two armchairs, a coffee table, a telephone with an answering machine, an extremely expensive and elaborate hi-fi set, and around the walls shelves to accommodate a great range of books (which are evidently cherished) and an extensive collection of records, in which Wagner and other opera sets can be distinguished.*

Stage left is a door that leads onto a small hall, at one end of which is the front door, and at the other a door which, in its turn, when opened, reveals a passage that goes onto stairs going down to the basement. More stairs lead up from the hall to another section of the house. The house has, in fact, recently been divided into two, so that there is a top flat.

Stage right has a door that leads to the kitchen, and as becomes evident, there is a door that opens from the kitchen into the garden.

When the curtain goes up, SIMON *is unwrapping a new record. He takes it out with the air of a man who is deeply looking forward to listening to it—there are several records, in fact—the complete Parsifal. He goes to the hi-fi, puts the first record on, listens, adjusts the level, then goes to the sofa and settles himself in it. The opening chords of Parsifal fill the theatre.*

The door opens, left. DAVE *enters.* SIMON *turns, looks at him, concealing his irritation as* DAVE *wanders into the kitchen, returns, and sits restlessly in the armchair. A pause in the music.*

DAVE. What's that then?

SIMON *gets up and switches off the record.*

SIMON. Wagner. Do you like him?

DAVE (*standing up*). No, well I mean he was anti-semitic, wasn't he. Sort of early fascist, ego-manic type.

SIMON. What about his music, do you like that?

DAVE. Well, I mean, I'm not likely to like his music if I don't like his type, am I?

SIMON (*concealing his impatience*). Everything all right? In the flat, that is. No complaints or other urgencies?

DAVE. No, no, that's all right. Oh, you mean about the rent?

SIMON. Good God no, I wasn't thinking about the rent.

DAVE. It's all right if it waits a bit then, is it?

SIMON. Good God yes, pay us this week's when you pay us last week's—next week, or whenever.

DAVE. OK. I'm a bit short, you know how it is. Your wife out again then?

SIMON. Yes, she's gone to (*thinks*) Salisbury. She left last night.

DAVE. That girl in the first year came round last night for something to eat. I dropped down to borrow a chop or something, fish fingers would have done.

SIMON. Would they really?

DAVE. But she wasn't here, your wife.

SIMON. No, she wouldn't have been, as she was either in, or on her way to, Salisbury.

DAVE. So I had to take her out for a kebab and some wine. Then I had to get her to come back.

SIMON. Ah, she stayed the night then? Good for you!

DAVE. No, she didn't.

SIMON. Oh. You managed to get rid of her, then, instead, well done!

DAVE. She just left by herself.

SIMON. Before you had a chance to get rid of her, oh dear, why?

DAVE. Said she didn't fancy me.

SIMON. Good God, why ever not?

DAVE. I don't know. I mean I asked her if she'd like a screw and she said no. Then I asked her why not, and she said she didn't fancy me, that was why not.

SIMON. Still, she's left the door open for a platonic relationship.

DAVE. Yeah, well, then she went off to see something on television with some friend. I haven't got a television.

SIMON. Well, I'm afraid I can't help you there, nor have we.

DAVE. Anyway she said she might be going to that Marxist bookshop down the road today.

SIMON. What time?

DAVE. About lunch time, she said.

SIMON. But good God, lunch will soon be on you, hadn't you better get going—it would be tragic to miss her.

DAVE. Yeah, well that's it, you see. I'm a bit short, like I said. I mean we can't do anything—

Pause.

SIMON. Can I lend you some?

DAVE. What?

SIMON. Can I lend you some money?

DAVE. Yeah, OK.

SIMON (*giving him a fiver*). Is that enough?

DAVE. Yeah. Right. (*Takes it.*) That's five.

SIMON. Well, I'll get back to my music while you're making your own.

STEPHEN (*enters, through the kitchen door*). Hello. Oh hello.

SIMON (*concealing his dismay*). Oh, Stephen. This is Dave, who's taken over the upstairs flat. Dave, my brother Stephen.

STEPHEN. Oh yes, you're at the Poly, aren't you?

DAVE. That's right.

STEPHEN. What are you studying?

DAVE. Sociology.

STEPHEN. That must be jolly interesting. What aspect?

DAVE. What?

STEPHEN. Of sociology.

DAVE. Oh, the usual stuff.

STEPHEN. Psychology, statistics, politics, philosophy, I suppose.

DAVE. We're sitting in at the moment.

STEPHEN. Really? Why?

DAVE. Oh, usual sort of thing. Well—(*Goes towards the door and out.*)

STEPHEN. What is the usual sort of thing?

SIMON. No idea.

STEPHEN (*after a pause*). Well, I must say!

SIMON. Oh, he's not as thick as he seems.

STEPHEN. Isn't he? He certainly seems quite thick. (*Sits down.*) I'm surprised a student could afford that flat, what do you charge him?

SIMON. Two pounds a week, I think.

STEPHEN. But you could get, good Heavens, even through the rent tribunal, ten times that.

SIMON. Oh, we're not out to make money from it.

STEPHEN. Well, *he* seems rather an odd choice for your charity, with so many others in real need. Beth's not here, then?

SIMON. No, she's taken some of her foreign students to Canterbury.

STEPHEN. Did she go with that teacher she was telling Teresa about?

SIMON. Chap called Ned?

STEPHEN. Yes.

SIMON. Yes.

STEPHEN. What do you think of him?

SIMON. Oh, rather a wry, sad little fellow. Bit of a failure, I'd say, from what I've seen of him.

STEPHEN. A failure? In what way?

SIMON. Oh, you know, teaching English to foreigners.

STEPHEN. So does Beth.

SIMON. True, but Beth isn't a middle-aged man with ginger hair, a pigeon-toed gait, a depressed-looking wife and four children to boot.

STEPHEN. You know, sometimes I can't help wondering how

people describe me. A middle-aged public school teacher with five children to boot. A bit of a failure too, eh? Anyhow, that's how I feel today.

SIMON. Why, what's the matter?

STEPHEN. That damned interview.

SIMON. Interview?

STEPHEN. For the Assistant Headmastership. You'd forgotten then!

SIMON. No, no of *course* I hadn't. When is it exactly?

STEPHEN (*looks at him*). Yesterday.

SIMON. Good God! Was it really? Well, what happened?

STEPHEN. I didn't get it.

SIMON. Well, who did?

STEPHEN. A chap called MacGregor. And quite right too, as he's already Assistant Headmaster of a small public school in Edinburgh, very capable, written a couple of text books—in other words he's simply the better man for the job.

SIMON. I don't see what that's got to do with it. I don't know how your Headmaster had the face to tell you.

STEPHEN. Oh, he didn't. Nobody's had the face or the grace. Yet.

SIMON. Then how do you know he's got it.

STEPHEN. It was written all over MacGregor. I've never seen anyone so perky after an interview.

SIMON. Oh good God, is that all? Of course he was perky. He's a Scot isn't he? They're always perky. Except when they're doleful. Usually they're both at once.

STEPHEN. If you'd seen him come bouncing down the library steps.

SIMON. In my experience a bouncing candidate is a rejected candidate. No, no, Steve, my money's on your paddle feet. (*He sits.*)

STEPHEN. Even though my interview lasted a mere half hour although his lasted fifty-seven minutes? Even though I fluffed my mere half hour, and before a hostile board. Do you know, one of the Governors couldn't get over the fact that I'd taken my degree at Reading. He was unable to grasp that Reading was a university even, he referred to it as if it were some cutprice institution where I'd scraped up some—some diploma on the cheap. MacGregor went to Oxford, needless to say.

SIMON. Did he? Which college?

STEPHEN. And then another Governor harped on the number of our children—he kept saying *five* children, eh? Like that. Five children, eh? As if I'd had—I don't know—five—five—

SIMON. Cheques returned.

STEPHEN. What?

SIMON. That's what you made it sound as if he sounded as if he were saying.

STEPHEN. Anyway, there were the two Governors manifestly hostile.

SIMON. Out of how many?

STEPHEN. Two.

SIMON. Ah, but then your Headmaster was on your side.

STEPHEN. Perhaps. (*Pause.*) At least until I succeeded in putting him off.

SIMON. How?

STEPHEN. By doing something I haven't done since I was twelve years old.

SIMON (*after a pause*). Can you be more specific?

STEPHEN. You will of course laugh, for which I shan't of course blame you, but I'm not sure that I can stand it if you do laugh at the moment. It was something very trivial, but also very embarrassing. (*Pause.*) You see, the Governor who didn't feel Reading was up to snuff had a rather low, husky voice, and towards the end I bent forward, rather sharply, to catch something he said, and this movement caused me to fart.

They stare levelly at each other. SIMON's face is completely composed.

SIMON. You haven't farted since you were twelve?

STEPHEN. In public, I meant.

SIMON. Oh. Loudly?

STEPHEN. It sounded to me like a pistol shot.

SIMON. The question, of course, is what it sounded like to Headmaster.

STEPHEN. Like a fart, I should think.

SIMON. Oh, he probably found it sympathetically human, you've no grounds for believing he'd hold anything so accidental against you, surely?

STEPHEN. I don't know, I simply don't know. (*He gets up.*) But afterwards when he had us around for some of his wife's herbal coffee—

SIMON. Herbal coffee?

STEPHEN. They paid far more attention to MacGregor than they did to me. I had to struggle to keep my end up. Headmaster was distinctly aloof in his manner—and MacGregor, of course, was relaxed and I suppose a fair man would call it charming.

SIMON. What herbs does she use?

STEPHEN. What? What's that got to do with it? How would I know.

SIMON. Sorry, I was just trying to imagine the—the setting, so to speak.

STEPHEN. You know, what really hurts is that I can't complain that it's unfair. MacGregor really is better qualified, quite obviously an admirable bloke. But what I do resent, and can't help resenting, is the edge Oxford gives him—the simple fact that he went there improves his chances—but I suppose that's the way of the world, isn't it? Almost everybody goes along with it, don't they?

SIMON. Oh, I don't know—

STEPHEN. Of course you know. You subscribe to it yourself, don't you?

SIMON. Certainly not. Why should I?

STEPHEN. Because you went to Oxford yourself.

SIMON. Good God, so what?

STEPHEN. Well, how many other members of your editorial board also went there?

SIMON. Only five.

STEPHEN. Out of how many?

SIMON. Eight.

STEPHEN. And where did the other three go, Cambridge?

SIMON. Only two of them.

STEPHEN. And so only *one* of the nine went elsewhere?

SIMON. No, he didn't go anywhere. He's the Chairman's son.

STEPHEN. I think that proves my point.

SIMON. It proves merely that our editorial board is composed
of Oxford and Cambridge graduates, and a half-wit. It proves
absolutely nothing about your chances of beating MacDonald
to the Assistant Headmastership. And it's my view that poor
old MacDonald, whether he be Oxford MacDonald or
Cambridge MacDonald or Reading MacDonald or plain
Edinburgh MacDonald—

STEPHEN. MacGregor.

SIMON. What?

STEPHEN. His name happens to be MacGregor.

SIMON. Absolutely. Has no chance at all. Even if they do
believe you have too few qualifications and too many
children, even if they suspect that your single fart heralds
chronic incontinence, they'll still have to appoint you. And if
they've been extra courteous to MacDonald it's only to
compensate him for coming all the way from Edinburgh for a
London rebuff. (*Stands up.*)

STEPHEN. Actually it would be better, if you don't mind, not
to try and jolly me along with reasons and reassurances. I
shall have to face the disappointment sooner or later, and I'd
rather do it sooner—wouldn't you?

SIMON. No, I have a distinct preference for later, myself. I
really do think you'll get it you know.

STEPHEN. Yes, well thanks anyway. I'd better get back. What
time's your friend coming?

SIMON. What friend?

STEPHEN. When I phoned and asked whether I could come
round, you said it mightn't be worth my while as you were
expecting a friend.

SIMON. Good God! Yes. Still, he's one of those people who

never turns up when expected. So if I remember to expect him I should be all right.

STEPHEN. You mean you don't want him to turn up? Who is he anyway?

SIMON. Jeff Golding.

STEPHEN. Oh *him!* Yes, well I must say that piece he wrote in one of last week's Sundays, on censorship and children—I've never read anything so posturingly half-baked.

SIMON. Oh, I doubt if he was posturing, he really is half-baked.

STEPHEN. I shall never forget—never—how he ruined the dinner party—the one time I met him—his drunkenness and his appalling behaviour. And I shall particularly never forget his announcing that people—he meant me, of course—only went into public school teaching because they were latent pederasts.

SIMON. Good God, what did you say?

STEPHEN. I told him to take it back.

SIMON. And did he?

STEPHEN. He offered to take back the latent, and congratulated me on my luck. That was his idea of badinage. By God I don't often lose control but I made a point of cornering him in the hall when he was leaving. I got him by the lapels and warned him that I'd a good mind to beat some manners into him. If Teresa hadn't happened to come out of the lavatory just then—she'd rushed in there in tears—I might have done him some damage. I've never told you that bit before, have I?

SIMON. You haven't told me any of it before, it's very amusing. Tell me, who gave this memorable dinner party?

STEPHEN. You did.

SIMON. Did I really? I don't remember it. It must have been a long time ago.

STEPHEN. Yes, but I have a feeling your friend Jeff Golding will remember it all right.

The front door slams and JEFF GOLDING *enters left.*

JEFF. Simon—ah, there you are.

There is a pause.

Weren't you expecting me?

SIMON. I most certainly was. Oh, my brother Stephen—Jeff Golding. I believe you know each other.

STEPHEN. We do indeed.

JEFF. Really? Sorry, 'fraid I don't remember.

STEPHEN. A dinner party Simon gave—some years ago.

JEFF (*clearly not remembering at all*). Nice to see you again. Could I have a scotch please? (*To* SIMON.)

SIMON. Of course. (*Goes to the drinks table.*) Steve?

STEPHEN. No thank you.

JEFF (*collapses into a chair*). Christ! Christ! I've just had a session at the Beeb, taping a piece with Bugger Lampwith. I've got the goods on him at last.

STEPHEN. Lampwith. Isn't he a poet?

JEFF. Not even. He's an Australian. A closet Australian. Went to Oxford instead of Earl's Court. Thinks it makes him one of us. Still, I got him out of his closet with his vowels around his tonsils, once or twice. Thrice, actually. (*Laughs at the recollection.*)

STEPHEN. What exactly have you got against him?

JEFF. Isn't that enough?

STEPHEN. Simply that he's an Australian?

JEFF. They're all right as dentists.

STEPHEN. But could you please explain to me why you have it in for Australians.

JEFF. Once you let them into literature they lower the property values.

STEPHEN. Really? How?

JEFF. They're too fertile, scribble, scribble, scribble like little Gibbons. They breed whole articles out of small reviews, don't mind what work they do, go from sports journalists to movie critics to novelists to poets to television pundits, and furthermore they don't mind how little they get paid as long as they fill our space. So you see if there weren't any Australians around sods like me wouldn't end up having to flog our crap to the Radio Times and even the Shiterary Supplement, let alone spend Saturday morning interviewing buggers like Bugger Lampwith.

STEPHEN. We've got half a dozen Australian boys in our school at the moment. They're not only friendly, frank and outgoing, they're also intelligent and very hard-working.

JEFF. Exactly, the little buggers. Hey! (*To* SIMON.) Roger's been going around telling people I can't face him since my review of his turgid little turd of a novel. Have you read it?

SIMON. Which?

JEFF. My review—first things first.

SIMON. Yes, I did.

JEFF. Well?

SIMON. Some good jokes, I thought.

JEFF. Weren't there? And what did you honestly, frankly and actually think of his turd?

SIMON. I haven't read it.

JEFF. Didn't you publish it?

SIMON. Yes.

JEFF. Well, if you ask me, the blokie you got to write the blurb hadn't read it either, bloody sloppy piece of crap, who did it anyway?

SIMON. Actually I did.

JEFF. D'you know what it bloody is—I'll tell you what it bloody is—I wish I'd come out with it straight when I wrote about it—it's a piece of—*literature,* that's what it bloody is!

STEPHEN. You don't like literature?

JEFF (*a pause*). I don't like literature, no.

STEPHEN. Why not?

JEFF. Because it's a bloody boring racket.

STEPHEN. You think literature is a *racket?*

JEFF. Are you in it too?

STEPHEN. I happen to teach it, it so happens.

JEFF. Does it, Christ! To whom?

STEPHEN. Sixth formers. At Amplesides.

JEFF. What's Amplesides?

STEPHEN. It happens to be a public school.

JEFF. Does it? Major or minor?

STEPHEN. Let's just say that it's a good one, if you don't mind.

JEFF. I don't mind saying it even if it's not. It's a good one. Christ, can't remember when I last met a public school teacher.

STEPHEN. Probably when you last met me.

JEFF. But I don't remember that, don't forget.

STEPHEN. Would you like me to remind you? I'm the latent
pederast.

JEFF (*after a pause*). Then you're in the right job.

STEPHEN (*to* SIMON). I think I'd better go. Before I do
something I regret. (*Turns and goes out through kitchen.*)

SIMON. Oh right. (*Making an attempt to follow* STEPHEN.)
Love to Teresa and the kids. (*Calling it out.*)

Sound of doors slamming. JEFF *helps himself to another
scotch.*

JEFF. Seems a real sweetie, what's he like in real life?

SIMON. Not as stupid as he seems.

JEFF. That still leaves him a lot of room to be stupid in.

SIMON. He *is* my brother.

JEFF. I'm very sorry.

SIMON. Actually, the last time he met you, he offered to fight
you.

JEFF. Then he's matured since then. Where's Beth?

SIMON. Gone to Canterbury.

JEFF. With her woggies?

SIMON. Yes.

JEFF. Never seem to see her these days. You two still all right, I
take it?

SIMON. Yes, thanks.

JEFF. Christ, you're lucky, don't know how you do it. She's so
bloody attractive of course, as well as nice and intelligent. I
suppose that helps.

SIMON. Yes, it does really.

JEFF. And she's got that funny little moral streak in her—she doesn't altogether approve of me, I get the feeling. Even after all these years. Christ, women! Listen there's something I want to talk to you about, and I'll just lay down the guide-lines of your response. What I want from you is an attentive face and a cocked ear, the good old-fashioned friendly sympathy and concern for which you're celebrated, O bloody K?

SIMON. Well, I'll do my best.

JEFF. Remember Gwendoline?

SIMON. Gwendoline, no. Have I met her?

JEFF. Hundreds of times.

SIMON. Really, where?

JEFF. With me.

SIMON. Oh. Which one was she—to tell you the truth, Jeff, there've been so many that the only one I still have the slightest recollection of is your ex-wife.

JEFF. Are you sure?

SIMON. Absolutely.

JEFF. Well, that was Gwendoline.

SIMON. Oh, I thought her name was Gwynyth.

JEFF. Why?

SIMON. What?

JEFF. Why should you think her name was Gwynyth?

SIMON. Wasn't she Welsh?

JEFF. No, she bloody was not Welsh.

SIMON. Well, I haven't seen her years, don't forget, not since

the afternoon you threw your drink in her face and walked out
on her.

JEFF. And that's all you remember?

SIMON. Well, it *did* happen in my flat, a lunch party you asked
me to give so that you could meet the then Arts Editor of the
Sunday Times, and you did leave her sobbing on my bed, into
my pillow, with the stink of scotch everywhere—

JEFF. Don't you remember anything else about my Gwendoline
days, for Christ's sake? What I used to tell you about her?

SIMON (*thinks*). Yes. You used to tell me that she was the
stupidest woman I'd ever met.

JEFF. *You'd* ever met.

SIMON. Yes.

JEFF. And was she?

SIMON. Yes.

JEFF. Well, you've met some stupider since, haven't you?

SIMON. Probably, but fortunately I can't remember them
either.

JEFF. So you rather despised my poor old Gwendoline, did
you?

SIMON. Absolutely. So did you.

JEFF. Then why do you think I married her?

SIMON. Because of the sex.

JEFF. Did I tell you that too?

SIMON. No, you told her that, once or twice, in front of me.

JEFF. Christ, what a bloody swine of a fool I was. (*Pours
himself another drink.*) Well, now I'm suffering for it, aren't

I? Listen, a few months ago I bumped into her in Oxford
Street. I hadn't given her a thought in all that time, and
suddenly there we were, face to face, looking at each other.
For a full minute just looking. And do you know something,
she cried. And I felt as if we were—Christ, you know—still
married. But in the very first days of it, when we couldn't keep
our hands off each other. In a matter of minutes.

SIMON. Minutes?

JEFF. Minutes. Bloody minutes. All over each other.

SIMON. In *Oxford* Street.

JEFF. I'll tell you—I put my hand out, very slowly, and stroked
her cheek. The tears were running down, her mouth was
trembling—and she took my hand and pressed it against her
cheek. Then I took her to Nick's flat—he's still in hospital by
the way.

SIMON. Really? I didn't know he'd gone in.

JEFF. They're trying aversion therapy this time, but it won't do
any good. He's so bloody addictive that he'll come out hooked
on the cure and still stay hooked on the gin, poor sod. Saline
chasers. Anyway, I took her to Nick's, and had her, and had
her, and had her. Christ! And when she left what do you think
I did?

SIMON. Slept, I should think.

JEFF. I cried, that's what I did. Didn't want her to leave me,
you see. I'm in love with her. I think I love her. And since
then there have been times when I've thought I even liked her.
Well?

SIMON. Well Jeff, that's marvellous. Really marvellous.

JEFF. Oh yes, bloody marvellous to discover that you want to
marry your ex-wife.

SIMON. But why ever not? It just confirms that you were right
the first time. Why not marry her?

JEFF (*taking another drink*). Because she's got a new bloody husband, that's why. In fact not so new, five years old. A bloody don in Cambridge called Manfred. Christ knows why he had to go and *marry* her!

SIMON. Perhaps he likes sex too.

JEFF. According to Gwen he likes TV situation comedies, football matches, wrestling, comic books, horror films and sadistic thrillers, but not sex.

SIMON. What does he teach?

JEFF. Moral sciences.

SIMON. Then there's your answer. Philosophers have a long tradition of marrying stupid women, from Socrates on. They think it clever. Does she love him?

JEFF. Of course she does, she loves everyone. But she loves me most. Except for their bloody child. She bloody dotes on the bloody child.

SIMON. Oh. How old is it?

JEFF. Two—three—four—that sort of age.

SIMON. Boy or girl?

JEFF. Can't really tell. The one time I saw it, through my car window, it was trotting into its nursery school with its arm over its face, like a mobster going to the grand jury.

SIMON. Haven't you asked Gwen which it is?

JEFF. Yes, but only to show interest. Anyway, what does it matter, what matters is she won't leave Manfred because of it. She's *my* wife, not his, I had her first, and she admits as much, she'll always be mine, but all I get of her is two goes a week when I drive up to Cambridge—Tuesdays and Thursdays in the afternoon when Manfred's conducting seminars. In the rooms of some smartie-boots theologian.

SIMON (*pacing up and down*). Do you mean Manfred conducts his seminars in the rooms of some smartie-boots theologian or you have Gwen in the rooms of some smartie-boots theologian?

JEFF. I have Gwen there. He's friend of Manfred's you see.

SIMON. So Manfred's asked him to let you use his rooms?

JEFF. Oh no, Manfred doesn't know anything about it. Or about me. No, smartie-boots seems to have some idea that it's part of his job to encourage what he calls sin. Oh Christ, you know the type, a squalid little Anglican queen of a pimp the little sod. Turns my stomach. (*Adds more scotch.*) Christ, you know, Simon, you want to know something about me?

SIMON. What? (*Sinks into an armchair.*)

JEFF. I'm English, yes, English to my marrow's marrow. After years of buggering about as a cosmopolitan literateur, going to PEN conferences in Warsaw, hob-nobbing with Frog poets and Eyetye essayists, German novelists and Greek composers, I suddenly realise I hate the lot of them. Furthermore I detest women, love men, loathe queers. D'you know when I'm really at bloody peace with myself? When I'm caught in a traffic jam on an English road, under an English heaven—somewhere between London and Cambridge, on my way to Gwen, on my way back from her, rain sliding down the window, engine humming, dreaming—dreaming of what's past or is to come. Wrapped in the anticipation or the memory, no, the anticipation *of* the memory. (*Pause.*) Oh Christ—it's my actual bloody opinion that this sad little, bloody little country of ours is finished at last. Bloody finished at last. Yes, it truly is bloody well actually finished at last. I mean that. Had the VAT man around the other day. That's what we get now instead of the muffin man. I remember the muffin men, I'm old enough to remember the muffin men. Their bells and smells and lighting of the lamps—do you remember?

Sometimes I even remember hansom cabs and crinoline, the music halls and Hobbes and Sutcliffe . . . (*Smiles.*) Or the memory of the anticipation, I suppose. Stu Lampwith. Christ, the bugger! (*Pause.*) Well Christ—I suppose I'd better go and write my piece. (*He gets to his feet.*) Did I tell you what that cold-hearted bitch said last night, in bed? Christ!

SIMON. Who?

JEFF. What?

SIMON. What cold-hearted bitch?

JEFF. Davina. (*Takes another scotch.*)

SIMON. Davina?

JEFF. You don't know about Davina?

SIMON (*wearily*). No.

JEFF. You haven't met her?

SIMON. No, no—I don't think—

JEFF. But Christ, I've got to tell you about bitch Davina. (*Sits down.*)

SIMON. Why?

JEFF. Because she is actually and completely the most utterly and totally—(*Lifts his hand.*)

There is a ring at the door-bell.

What?

SIMON. Just a minute, Jeff. (*Goes to the door, opens it.*)

DAVINA. Hello, is Jeff here, by any chance? (JEFF *groans in recognition and sits down on the sofa.*)

SIMON. Yes, yes he is. Come in.

(DAVINA *enters.* JEFF *ignores her.*)

DAVINA. I'm Davina Saunders. (*To* SIMON.)

SIMON. I'm Simon Hench.

DAVINA. I know.

There is a pause.

SIMON. Would you like a drink?

DAVINA. Small gin and bitters, please.

SIMON *goes across to the drinks table.*

JEFF. How did you know I was here?

DAVINA. You said you would be.

JEFF. Why did I tell you?

DAVINA. Because I asked you.

JEFF. But why did I tell you. Because you see, I wanted a quiet conversation with my friend, Simon, you see.

DAVINA. You're all right then, are you?

JEFF. What? (*A pause.* SIMON *brings* DAVINA *her drink.*)

DAVINA. How did the interview go?

JEFF. All right.

DAVINA. What's he like?

JEFF. Who?

DAVINA. Bugger Lampwith.

JEFF. OK.

DAVINA. What's OK about him?

JEFF. He's all right.

DAVINA. Good.

JEFF. What do you mean, good?

DAVINA. That he's all right. (*Sits down.*)

JEFF. Well, what d'you want me to say, you follow me across bloody London, you turn up when I'm having a private bloody conversation with my old friend Simon, you're scarcely in the room before you ask me whether I'm drunk—

DAVINA. As a matter of sober precision, I did not ask you whether you were drunk. I asked you whether you were all right.

JEFF. Then as a matter of drunken precision, no, I'm not all right, I'm drunk.

DAVINA. That's surprising, as with you being all right and being drunk are usually precisely synonymous.

JEFF. But now you're here, aren't you, and that alters everything, doesn't it?

DAVINA. Does it?

JEFF. I thought you were going to spend the morning at the British Bloody Museum. I thought we'd agreed not to see each other for a day or two, or even a year or two—

There is a pause.

SIMON. What are you doing at the BM, some research?

JEFF. That's what she's doing. On Major Bloody Barttelot. Got the idea from *my* review of that Life of Stanley—naturally.

SIMON. Really, and who is Major Bloody Barttelot?

DAVINA. Major Barttelot went with Stanley to the Congo, was left in a camp to guard the Rear Column, and ended up flogging, shooting, and even, so the story goes, eating the natives.

JEFF. Pleasant work for a woman, eh?

SIMON. Major Barttelot was a *woman?*

DAVINA. He was an English gentleman. Although he did find it pleasant work from what I've discovered, yes.

SIMON. Really? And are you planning a book?

JEFF. Of course she is, cannibalism, sadism, doing down England all at the same time, how can it miss? Why do you think she's on to it?

SIMON. I must say it sounds quite fascinating. Who's your publisher?

DAVINA. I haven't got one yet.

JEFF. Is that what summoned you away from the BM, the chance of drawing up a contract with my old friend, the publisher Simon? (*Refills his glass.*)

DAVINA. Actually, I haven't been to the BM this morning. I've been on the telephone. And what summoned me here was first that I wanted to give you your key back. (*Throws it over to him.*)

JEFF (*makes no attempt to catch it*). Thank you.

DAVINA. And secondly to tell you about the telephone call.

JEFF. What? Who was it?

DAVINA. Your ex-wife's husband. Manfred.

JEFF. What did he want?

DAVINA. You.

JEFF. Why?

DAVINA. He wanted you to know the contents of Gwendoline's suicide letter.

JEFF (*after a pause*). What? Gwendoline—what—Gwen's dead!

SIMON. Good God!

DAVINA. No.

JEFF. But she tried—tried to commit suicide?

DAVINA. Apparently.

JEFF. What do you mean apparently, you mean she failed?

DAVINA. Oh, I'd say she succeeded. At least to the extent that Manfred was hysterical, I had a wastefully boring morning on the telephone, and you look almost sober. What more could she expect from a mere bid, after all?

JEFF. For Christ sake, what happened, what actually happened?

DAVINA. Well, Manfred's narrative was a trifle rhapsodic.

JEFF. But you said there was a letter.

DAVINA. He only read out the opening sentences—he was too embarrassed by them to go on.

JEFF. Embarrassed by what?

DAVINA. Oh, Gwendoline's epistolary style, I should think. It was rather shaming.

JEFF. Look, where is she?

DAVINA. In that hospital in Cambridge probably. And if you're thinking of going up there, you should reflect that Manfred is looking forward to beating you to a pulp. A *bloody* pulp was his phrase, and unlike yourself he seems to use the word literally, rather than for rhetorical effect or as drunken punctuation. I like people who express themselves limpidly (*to* SIMON) under stress, don't you?

JEFF (*throws his drink at her, splashing her blouse, etc.*). Is that limpid enough for you?

DAVINA. No, tritely theatrical, as usual. But if you're absolutely determined to go, and you might as well because what else have you to do? I advise you not to drive. Otherwise you may have to make do with one of the hospitals *en route.*

SIMON. Yes, you really shouldn't drive, Jeff . . .

JEFF *turns, goes out, left, slamming the door. There is a pause.*

I'll get you something to wipe your shirt—

DAVINA. Don't bother, it's far too wet. But another drink please. (*Hands him her glass.*)

SIMON. Of course.

Takes it, goes to the drinks table.
DAVINA *takes off her shirt and throws it over a chair. She is bra-less. She goes to the large wall mirror, and dries herself with a handkerchief from her bag.*
SIMON *turns with the drink, looks at* DAVINA, *falters slightly, then brings her her drink.*

DAVINA. God, what a stupid man, don't you think?

SIMON. Well, a bit excitable at times, perhaps.

DAVINA. No, stupid really, and in an all-round way. You know, when I was at Oxford one used to take his articles quite seriously—not very seriously but quite. But now of course one sees that his facility, though it may pass in the Arts pages as intelligence and originality, was something merely cultivated in late adolescence for the examination halls. He hasn't developed, in fact his Gwendoline syndrome makes it evident that he's regressed. Furthermore his drunken bravado quickly ceases to be amusing, on top of which he's a fourth-rate fuck.

SIMON. Oh well, perhaps he's kind to animals.

DAVINA (*sitting on the sofa*). To think I thought he might be of some use to me. But of course he's out of the habit, if he was ever in it, of talking to women who like to think and therefore talk concisely, for whom intelligence does actually

involve judgement, and for whom judgement concludes in
discrimination. Hence the appeal, I suppose, of a pair of tits
from which he can dangle, with closed eyes and infantile
gurglings. Especially if he has to get to them furtively, with a
sense of not being allowed. Yes, stupid, don't you agree?

SIMON. Did you really go to Oxford?

DAVINA. Came down two years ago, why?

SIMON. From your style you sound more as if you went to
Cambridge.

DAVINA. Anyway, he's nicely gone, you will admit, and four
bad weeks have been satisfactorily concluded.

SIMON. Aren't you a little worried about him, though?

DAVINA. Why should I be?

SIMON. Well, Manfred did threaten to beat him to a bloody
pulp, after all. And it may not be an idle boast. Men whose
wives attempt suicide because of other men sometimes become
quite animated, even if they are moral scientists.

DAVINA. Oh, I think the wretched Manfred will be more
bewildered than belligerent. I composed that fiction between
Great Russell Street and here. Of course I didn't know until I
met his glassy gaze and received his boorish welcome whether
I was actually going to work it through. It was quite thrilling,
don't you think?

SIMON. You mean, Gwendoline didn't try to commit suicide?

DAVINA. Surely you don't imagine that *that* complacent old
cow would attempt even an attempted suicide?

SIMON. Why did you do it?

DAVINA. Spite of course. Well, he told me he wanted to bring
it all to a climax, although he wanted no such thing of course,
prolonged and squalid messes that lead least of all to climaxes

being his method, so my revenge has been to provide him with one that should be exactly in character—prolonged, squalid and utterly messy even by Cambridge standards, don't you think? *You're* married, aren't you? To Beth, isn't it?

SIMON. That's right.

DAVINA. I've only just realized she isn't here, is she?

SIMON. Well, I suppose that's better than just realizing she was, isn't it?

DAVINA. I'd like to have met her. I've heard a great deal about you both, you mainly, of course. Are you two as imperturbably, not to say implacably *married* as he and everyone else says?

SIMON. I hope so.

DAVINA. And that you've never been unfaithful to Beth, at least as far as Jeff knows.

SIMON. Certainly never that far.

DAVINA. Don't you even fancy other women?

SIMON (*sits in the armchair*). My not sleeping with other women has absolutely nothing to do with not fancying them. Although I do make a particular point of not sleeping with women I don't fancy.

DAVINA. That's meant for me, is it?

SIMON. Good God, not at all.

DAVINA. You mean you do fancy me?

SIMON. I didn't mean that either.

DAVINA. But do you fancy me?

SIMON. Yes.

DAVINA. But you don't like me?

SIMON. No.

DAVINA. Ah, then do you fancy me *because* you don't like me? Some complicated set of manly mechanisms of that sort, is it?

SIMON. No, very simple ones that Jeff, for instance, would fully appreciate. I fancy you because of your breasts, you see. I'm revolted by your conversation and appalled by your behaviour. I think you're possibly the most egocentrically unpleasant woman I've ever met, but I have a yearning for your breasts. I'd like to dangle from them too, with my eyes closed and doubtless emitting infantile gurglings. Furthermore they look deceptively hospitable.

DAVINA. If they look deceptively hospitable, they're deceiving you. (*Comes over and sits on the arm of his chair.*) You're very welcome to a nuzzle. (*Pause.*) Go on then. And then we'll see what *you* can do.

SIMON *sits, hesitating for a moment, then gets up, gets* DAVINA's *shirt, hands it to her.*

Because of Beth?

SIMON. This is her house, as much as mine. It's *our* house, don't you see?

DAVINA. Fidelity means so much to you?

SIMON. Let's say rather more to me than a suck and a fuck with the likes of you. So, comes to that, does Jeff.

DAVINA. Yes, well I suppose that's to be expected in a friend of his. He doesn't begin to exist and nor do you.

SIMON. That's excellent. Because I haven't the slightest intention of letting you invent me.

DAVINA. And what about my Barttelot book?

SIMON. There I'm sure we shall understand each other. If it's any good, I shall be delighted to publish it. And if you've any sense, and you've got a hideous sight too much, you'll be delighted to let me. I shall give you the best advance available

in London, arrange an excellent deal with an American
publisher, and I shall see that it's edited to your advantage as
well as ours. If it's any good.

DAVINA. That means more to me than being sucked at and
fucked by the likes of you.

They smile. DAVINA *turns and goes out.*

SIMON, *with the air of a man celebrating, picks up the
keys and glasses, puts them away. Makes to go to the
gramophone, stops, goes to the telephone answering machine.*

SIMON (*records*). 348-0720, Simon Hench on an answering
machine. I shall be otherwise engaged for the rest of the day.
If you have a message for either myself or for Beth could you
please wait until after the high-pitched tone, and if that hasn't
put you off, speak. Thank you.

*Puts the button down, then goes over to the gramophone,
bends over to put a record on.*
DAVE *enters,* SIMON *freezes, turns.*

DAVE. She didn't show.

SIMON. What?

DAVE. Suzy. My girl. She didn't show. You know what I'd like
to do now, I'd like to get really pissed, that's what I'd like to
do.

SIMON. I don't blame you, and furthermore, why don't you?
You'll still catch the pubs if you hurry—

DAVE. Well, I'm a bit short, you see.

SIMON. But didn't you have a few pounds—

DAVE. Yeah, well I spent those.

SIMON. Oh, what on?

DAVE. Usual sort of stuff.

SIMON. Well then, let me. (*Pause.*) I've got just the thing.

Goes to the drinks table, fishes behind, takes out a bottle of Cyprus sherry.

Here. Go on, one of Beth's students gave it to her—it's yours. (*Hands it to* DAVE.) A Cyprus sherry. Nice and sweet. Now you settle down in some dark corner, with a receptacle by your side, and forget yourself completely. That's what I'd want to do if I were you. (*Points him towards the door.*)

DAVE *goes out.* SIMON *turns back to the hi-fi. Voices in the hall.*

DAVE (*opens the door*). Bloke here for you. (*Withdraws.*)

SIMON. What? (*Turns.*)

WOOD (*enters*). Mr. Hench?

SIMON. Yes.

WOOD. Can you spare me a few minutes? My name is Wood. Bernard Wood.

SIMON (*as if recognising the name, then checks it*). Oh?

WOOD. It means something to you, then?

SIMON. No, just an echo. Of Birnam Wood, it must be, coming to Dunsinane. No, I'm very sorry, it doesn't. Should it?

WOOD. You don't recognise me either, I take it?

SIMON. No, I'm afraid not. Should I?

WOOD. We went to school together.

SIMON. Did we really, Wundale?

WOOD. Yes. Wundale. I was all of three years ahead of you, but I recall you. It should be the other way around, shouldn't it? But then *you* were very distinctive.

SIMON. Was I really, in what way?

WOOD (*after a little pause*). Oh, as the sexy little boy that all the glamorous boys of my year slept with.

SIMON (*after a pause*). But you didn't?

WOOD. No.

SIMON. Well, I do hope you haven't come to make good, because it's too late, I'm afraid. The phase is over, by some decades. (*Little pause, then with an effort at courtesy.*) I'm sure I would have remembered you, though, if we had slept together.

WOOD. Well, perhaps your brother Stephen, isn't it? would remember me as we were in the same year, how is he?

SIMON. Oh, very well.

WOOD. Married, with children?

SIMON. Yes.

WOOD. And you're married?

SIMON. Yes.

WOOD. Good. Children?

SIMON. No.

WOOD. Why not?

SIMON. There's isn't enough room. What about you?

WOOD. Oh, as you might expect of someone like me. Married with children.

There is a pause.

SIMON. Well . . . um—you said there was something—?

WOOD. Yes, there is. It's of a rather personal—embarrassing nature.

Pause.

SIMON (*unenthusiastically*). Would a drink help?

WOOD. Oh, that's very kind. Some sherry would be nice, if you have it.

SIMON. Yes, I have it.

WOOD. Then some sherry, if I may.

SIMON. Yes, you may. (*Pours* WOOD *a sherry.*)

WOOD. My many thanks. Your very good health. I thought you might have heard my name the day before yesterday.

SIMON. Oh, in what context?

WOOD. From my girl, Joanna. In your office, at about six in the evening.

SIMON. Joanna?

WOOD. She came to see you about getting work in publishing. She's only just left art school, but you were kind enough to give her an appointment.

SIMON. Oh yes, yes. I do remember a girl—I'm terrible about names, a nice girl, I thought.

WOOD. Thank you. How did your meeting go? Just between us?

SIMON. Well, I thought she was really quite promising.

WOOD. But you didn't make her any promises.

SIMON. Well, no, I'm afraid I couldn't. What work of hers she showed me struck me as a—a trifle over-expressive for our needs. (*Pause.*) Why, is her version of our, um, talk different, in any way?

WOOD. She hasn't said anything about it at all.

SIMON. I see. And you've come to me to find out about her potential?

WOOD. Not really, no. I've come to ask you if you know where she is.

SIMON. Have you lost her then?

WOOD. She hasn't been home since I dropped her off at your office.

SIMON. Well, I'm very sorry, but I haven't seen her since she left my office.

WOOD. I only have one rule with her, that she come home at night. Failing that, that at least she let me know where or with whom she is spending the night. Failing that, that at least she telephone me first thing in the morning. Could I be more unreasonably reasonable? So before doing the rounds among her pals, from Ladbroke Grove to Earls Court, I thought it might be worth finding out from you if she let anything slip about her plans.

SIMON. Nothing that I can remember.

WOOD. She didn't mention any particular friend or boy-friend?

SIMON. Just the usual references to this drip and that drip in the modern manner. Look, from what one makes out of today's youth, isn't it likely that she'll come home when she feels in the mood or wants a good meal, eh?

WOOD. I suppose so.

SIMON. I can quite understand your worry—

WOOD. Can you? No, I don't think you can.

SIMON. No, perhaps not. But I really don't see how I can help you any further.

WOOD. Did you have it off with her?

SIMON. What? *What?*

WOOD. Did you have it off with her?

SIMON. Look, Wood, whatever your anxiety about your daughter, I really don't think, old chap, that you should insinuate yourself into people's homes and put a question like that to them. I mean, good God, you can't possibly expect me to dignify it with an answer, can you?

WOOD. In other words, you did.

SIMON (*after a long pause*). In other words, I'm afraid I did. Yes. Sorry, old chap.

Curtain.

Act Two

Curtain up on exactly same scene, WOOD *and* SIMON *in exactly the same postures. There is a pause.*

WOOD. Tell me, does your wife know you do this sort of thing?

SIMON. Why, are you going to tell her?

WOOD. Oh, I'm not a sneak. Besides, Joanna would never forgive me. She'd have told me herself, you know. She always does. She thinks it's good for me to know what she and her pals get up to. Do you do it often. (*Smiling.*)

SIMON. Reasonably often. Or unreasonably, depending on one's point of view.

WOOD. And always with girls of my Joanna's age?

SIMON. There or thereabouts, yes.

WOOD. Because you don't love your wife?

SIMON. No, because I do. I make a point, you see, of not sleeping with friends, or the wives of friends, or acquaintances even. No one in our circle. Relationships there can be awkward enough—

WOOD. It's a sort of code, is it?

SIMON. No doubt it seems a rather squalid one, to you.

WOOD. So that's why you chose my Joanna, is it?

SIMON. I didn't really choose her, you know. She came into my office, and we looked at her work, and talked—

WOOD. Until everybody else had gone. You decided, in other words, that she was an easy lay. And wouldn't make any fuss, afterwards.

SIMON. I also realized that I couldn't possibly do her any harm.

WOOD. What about the clap? (*Pause.*) I think I have right to know.

SIMON. I keep some pills at my office.

WOOD. So your post-coital period together was passed gobbling down anti-VD pills.

SIMON. One doesn't exactly gobble them—one swallows them, as one might digestive tablets.

WOOD. What about going back to your wife, reeking of sex?

SIMON. What?

WOOD. What do you do about the stench of your adulteries?

SIMON. I confess I find this enquiry into method rather depressing. I'd willingly settle for a burst of parental outrage—

WOOD. And I'd far rather satisfy my curiosity. Won't you please tell me?

SIMON. Very well. I stop off at my squash club, play a few points with the professional, then have a shower.

WOOD. But you don't suffer from any guilt afterwards? No post-coital distress, no angst or even embarrassment?

SIMON. Not unless this counts as afterwards.

WOOD. So really, only your sexual tastes have changed, your moral organism has survived intact since the days when you were that lucky sod, the Wundale Tart?

SIMON. Look, are you here because I slept around at thirteen, with the attractive boys of your year, or because I sleep

around with attractive girls of your daughter's generation, at
thirty-nine. Good God Wood, I'm beginning to find something
frankly Mediterranean in this obsession with your child's
sex-life and mine—after all, let's face it, in the grand
scheme of things, nothing much has happened, and in the
Anglo-Saxon scheme of things, your daughter's well over the
age of consent. That may sound brutal, but it's also true.

WOOD. Except in one important point. She's not my daughter.

SIMON. What? What is she then?

WOOD. My (*hesitates*) fiancée.

SIMON. Is it worth my saying sorry over again, or will my
earlier apologies serve. (*Pause.*) But I thought you said her
name was Wood—

WOOD. Yes.

SIMON. And your name is Wood.

WOOD. Yes, I changed my name as she refuses to change hers,
and won't marry me.

SIMON. In that case you're not Wood of Wundale.

WOOD. No, I'm Strapley—Strapley of Wundale. Known as
Wanker Strapley. Now do you remember me?

SIMON. Strapley—Strapley, Wanker Strapley. No.

WOOD. Well, your brother certainly would. He was known as
Armpits Hench. We were two of a kind, in that we were both
considered drips—what was the Wundale word for drip?

SIMON. I really can't remember.

WOOD. It was 'plop'.

SIMON. Plop.

WOOD. Those of us who were called it are more likely to
remember it than those of you who called us it. Plop. Yes, I'm

a plop, Hench. Whom one can now define, after so many years ploppily lived, as a chap who goes straight from masturbation to matrimony to monogamy.

SIMON. Oh, now there I think you're underestimating yourself. After all you have a wife, didn't you say, and now Joanna—

WOOD. I haven't got my wife any more. I doubt if I've got Joanna any more. But it's only appropriate that *you* should be the last common factor in our relationship. The first time I set eyes on her she reminded me of you.

SIMON. Where was that?

WOOD. At our local amateur theatricals. Joanna was playing in *The Winslow Boy*. She came on the stage in grey flannel bags, a white shirt and starched collar. She walked with a modest boy's gait, her eyes were wide with innocent knowledge. So did you walk down the Wundale Cloisters, that first year of yours. So I watched you then as I watched her. And there on my one side, were my two poor old sons, who've never reminded me of anyone but myself. And on the other, my poor old wife, the female plop, who from that second on ceased even to remind me that we shared a ploppy past. The years we'd spent together brooding over her mastoids, my haemorrhoids, and the mortgage on our maisonette, watching over our boys' sad little defeats, their failure to get into Wundale, their scrabbling for four O levels and then two A levels, their respective roles as twelfth man and scorer—they haven't even the competitiveness for sibling rivalry, poor old boys—all seemed, it all seemed such a waste, such a waste.

SIMON. But still you did succeed, to some extent at least, in breaking free. And you did succeed, to some extent I take it, with Joanna—so not altogether a case for predestination, when you think of it.

WOOD. Free meals, lots of gifts, little loans by the usual ploppy techniques of obligation and dependence—not that she felt dependent or obliged. She took what I offered and then asked for more. A generous nature. Did she get anything from you?

SIMON. She didn't ask for anything.

WOOD. Just as you never asked for anything from those boys—Higgens, Hornby, Darcy.

SIMON. It's true that Darcy was very kind with his truck, but I hope I never took it as payment, nor did he offer it as such.

WOOD (*pause*). What was it like with Joanna?

SIMON. Well, it was, um, I'm sure you know—she's a very uninhibited um—

WOOD. It was, then, satisfactory?

SIMON. Well, as these things go.

WOOD. They don't for me. I'm incapacitated by devotion.

SIMON. But you live together?

WOOD. She allows me to share the flat I've leased for her. We have different rooms—I sometimes sit on the side of her bed when she's in it. More often when she's not.

SIMON. You're obviously in the grip of a passion almost Dantesque in the purity of its hopelessness. You know, I really feel quite envious—for you every moment has its significance, however tortured, I just have to get by on my small pleasures and easy accommodations, my daily contentments—

WOOD. So she actually talks of me as a drip, does she?

SIMON. The ignorance of youth. Drips have neither your capacity for ironic self-castigation, nor more importantly your gift for the futile grand gesture.

WOOD. If she comes back, do you know what she'll do? She'll tell me about the boys she's slept with, the adults she's conned, the pot she's smoked. She'll tell me what a good time she had with you on your office floor—

SIMON. Sofa, actually.

WOOD. If she comes back. And I'll sit listening and yearning and just occasionally I'll soothe myself with the thought that one day she'll be dead, or even better old and unwanted and desperate—what I resent most about you, little Hench, is the way you seem to have gone on exactly as you promised you would at Wundale. If life catches up with everybody at the end, why hasn't it with you?

SIMON. But I haven't got to the end yet, thank God. I'm sure it will eventually.

WOOD. Sweet little Hench from Wundale, who picks off my Jo in an hour at his office, munches down a few pills, and then returns, without a worry in his head, the whole experience simply showered off, to his wife, who is doubtless quite attractive enough—is she?

SIMON. I find her quite attractive enough for me. Though taste in these matters—

WOOD. I'd like to kill you, Hench. Yes—kill you!

STEPHEN (enters through the kitchen). Si—(sees WOOD) Oh sorry, I didn't realise . . . Good God, it is, isn't it? Old Strapley, from Wundale?

WOOD. The name's Wood.

STEPHEN. Oh, sorry. You look rather like a chap who used to be at school with us, or rather me, in my year, Strapley.

WOOD. Really? What sort of chap was he?

STEPHEN. Oh actually, a bit of what we used to call a plop, wasn't he, Simon? So you're quite lucky not to be Strapley who almost certainly had a pretty rotten future before him. (Laughs.)

WOOD. Thank you for the sherry. (Turns quickly, goes out.)

SIMON. Not at all.

STEPHEN. I hope I haven't driven him off.

SIMON. Mmmm. Oh no, it's not you that's driven him off.

STEPHEN. What did he want?

SIMON. He was looking for somebody I once resembled. A case of mistaken identity, that's all.

STEPHEN. Well, if he had been Strapley, he'd hardly have changed at all, except that he's a quarter of a century older. Poor old Wanker Strapley. (*Sits down.*)

There is a pause.

Well Si, you were quite right, of course.

SIMON. Mmmm?

STEPHEN. I got it.

SIMON. Got what?

STEPHEN. The Assistant Headmastership.

SIMON. Oh. Oh good! (*Pause.*) Goody.

STEPHEN. You can imagine how stunned I was. I was so depressed when I got home, not only because I thought I'd lost the appointment, but because of that friend of yours—

SIMON. What friend?

STEPHEN. Golding. Jeff Golding. That he didn't even remember me, let alone what I'd threatened to do to him—and I could hear the children quarrelling in the garden, the baby crying in her cot, and when I sat down in the sitting-room there was a piece in *The Times* on the phasing out of public schools and private health, lumped together, and it all seemed—well! Then Teresa called out. I couldn't face her, you know how lowering her optimism can be—but I managed to drag myself into the kitchen—she had her back to me, at the oven, cooking up some nut cutlets for the children's lunch—and she said: 'Greetings, Assistant Headmaster of Amplesides.' Yes, Headmaster's wife had phoned while I was here, isn't that ironic? I could hardly believe it. So. I crammed down a nut cutlet—

SIMON. What was it like?

STEPHEN. What?

SIMON. The nut cutlet.

STEPHEN. Oh, it was from one of Headmaster's wife recipes. They're semi-vegetarian, you know.

SIMON. What did it *taste* like?

STEPHEN. Rather disgusting. But she's going to give us some more recipes if we like this one. Perhaps they'll be better.

SIMON. But you didn't like this one.

STEPHEN (*pause*). Aren't you pleased or even interested in my news?

SIMON. Of course I am.

STEPHEN. In spite of thinking MacDonald the better man? Well, you needn't worry about him, he's been offered a job too. As head of sixth form English.

SIMON. But you're head of sixth form English.

STEPHEN. Not any more. Headmaster reckons that with my new responsibilities I should step down from some of my teaching. I shall be head of fifth form English.

SIMON. Ah, fewer hours then.

STEPHEN. Actually more hours, but at fifth form level.

SIMON. Ah, less celebration. That's even better. So—(*loses thread, picks it up*) so justice has been done to two excellent candidates.

STEPHEN. I shall still be senior to MacDonald, you know.

SIMON. Isn't his name MacGregor?

STEPHEN. Yes. (*Little pause.*) Thanks, Si. (*Ironically.*)

SIMON. What for?

STEPHEN. Sharing my triumph with me.

SIMON. Why don't you—have a drink.

STEPHEN. No, thank you. Headmaster's asked Teresa to ask me to look in after lunch for a celebration glass.

SIMON. Oh. Of what?

STEPHEN. Pansy wine, I expect, as that's their favourite tipple.

SIMON (*after a pause*). Do they make it themselves?

STEPHEN. Headmaster's wife's aunt's husband does.

SIMON. Does he? (*Little pause.*) What's it like?

STEPHEN. You know what it's like.

SIMON. No, I don't. What's it like?

STEPHEN. Why do you want to know what it's like?

SIMON. Because I can't imagine what it's like, I suppose.

STEPHEN. Oh yes you can. Oh yes you can.

Turns, goes out through the kitchen. DAVE *enters left. He's slightly drunk. There is a pause.*

DAVE (*swaying slightly*). She's come. She's upstairs. She came all by herself.

SIMON. Who?

DAVE. That girl. Suzy. She dropped in for a cup of Nescafé.

SIMON. That's very good news, Dave. But should you, now

you've got her, leave her to have it all by herself. She sounds a highly-strung creature—

DAVE. Yeah, well the only thing is, I'm out of Nescafé.

SIMON. Oh.

DAVE. Well, have you got any, man?

SIMON. No, I'm sorry, we don't drink it.

DAVE. Anything else?

SIMON. Nothing at all like Nescafé, I'm afraid.

DAVE. What, no coffee at all?

SIMON. Oh yes, we've got coffee. But we use beans, a grinder, and a rather complicated filter process. Metal holders, paper cones—

DAVE. That'll do. Is it in the kitchen? (*He moves towards kitchen.*)

SIMON. Actually, it's rather a precious set.

DAVE. What? (*Returning.*)

SIMON. It's one of those few things I feel rather specially about.

DAVE. You mean you've got something against lending it to me?

SIMON. Not at all. The beans are in a sealed bag in an airtight tin—

DAVE. Oh yes you have. I can tell by your—your tone.

SIMON. My tone? Oh come now, Dave, that's only one possible gloss of my tone. No, you take the grinder, take the filters, the jug, the paper cones and the metal holders, and the coffee beans which come from a small shop in Holborn that keeps uncertain hours and can therefore be easily replaced with a great deal of difficulty, and don't addle your head with questions about my tone, good God! (*Pause.*) Go ahead. Please. (*Wearily.*)

DAVE. No thanks. No thank you! Because you do mind all right, you bloody mind all right.

SIMON. No, I don't.

DAVE. No, you don't, no, you don't bloody mind, do you—why should you, you've got it all already, haven't you? Machines for making coffee, a table covered with booze, crates of wine in your cellar, all the nosh you want, all the books you want, all the discs, the best hi-fi on the bloody market, taxis to work every morning, taxis home in the evening, a whole bloody house just for you and your sexy little wife—oh, you don't bloody mind anything you don't, what's there for you to mind, you shit you!

SIMON. Now that's not quite fair, Dave. It's not really a whole house, you know, since we converted the top floor at considerable expense and turned it over to you at an inconsiderable rent which you don't pay anyway. But then I don't mind that either.

DAVE. 'Course you bloody don't, why should you, you bloody like to run a pet, don't you, your very own special deserving case.

SIMON. I swear to you, Dave, I've never once thought of you as my pet or as a deserving case. If we'd wanted the former to occupy our upstairs flat we'd have got a monkey, and if we'd wanted the latter we'd have selected from among the unmarried mothers or the dispossessed old age pensioners. We thought quite hard about doing that, in fact.

DAVE. Then why didn't you?

SIMON. Because unmarried mothers mean babies, and babies mean nappies, and crying. While old age pensioners mean senility and eventual death.

DAVE. So I salve your bloody conscience without being a nuisance, eh? Right?

SIMON. Wrong. You salve my conscience by being a bloody nuisance. Your manners irritate me, your smell is unusually offensive, you're extremely boring, your sex-life is both depressing and disgusting, and you're a uniquely ungrateful cadge. But you really mustn't mind, because the point is that I don't, either. You have your one great value, that you run a poor third to recent births and imminent deaths.

DAVE. I'm not staying—I'm not staying—I'm not staying in the fucking top of your fucking house another fucking minute. You—you—(*Makes as if to hit* SIMON.)

SIMON *remains impassive.* DAVE *turns, goes out left. Noise of door slamming.* SIMON *closes door left. As he does so* STEPHEN *enters right.*

STEPHEN. It's sugary and tastes of onions. And it's quite revolting, just as you imagine.

SIMON. Well, I did imagine it would be revolting and probably sugary, but it never occurred to me it would taste of onions. But you can't have come back to report on its flavour already, you've only just left.

STEPHEN. I've been sitting in the car, thinking.

SIMON. What about?

STEPHEN. You, and your sneers. Oh, I don't altogether blame you, but I wish—(*sits down, looks at* SIMON) you'd had the guts to say it outright.

SIMON. Say what?

STEPHEN. That it's taken me twenty-four years to advance from Second Prefect of Wundale to Assistant Headmaster of Amplesides.

SIMON (*sitting down*). But that seems very respectable

progress to me. At that rate you should make it to Eton, if it still exists, by your mid-fifties. And as that's what you want, why should I have a word to say against it?

STEPHEN. Nor against the way I'm doing it? My stuffing down nut cutlets, and herbal coffee and pansy wine. And then coming back for seconds.

SIMON. But you do rather more than eat the inedible and drink the undrinkable. You're among the best Junior Colts football managers in the country.

STEPHEN. You despise my job.

SIMON. You've a family to support.

STEPHEN. So you do despise my job, and despise me for doing it. Why don't you say it. That's all I'm asking you to do.

SIMON. But I don't want to say it! I can't remember when you were last as you've been today, or what I said then to make you feel any better. I wish I could, because that's what I'd like to say now.

STEPHEN. The last time I felt like this eleven years ago, after Teresa had broken off our engagement, and you didn't say anything to make me feel any better. What you did say was that I was well out of it.

SIMON. Well, as you've been back in it for eleven years, you'll agree that it has little relevance now.

STEPHEN. It had little relevance then either. As I was desperately in love with her.

SIMON. Good God, all I probably meant, and I don't even remember saying it, was that if she didn't want to marry you then it was better to be out of it before the wedding.

STEPHEN. Oh no, oh no, all you meant was that *you* were relieved to be out of it.

SIMON. Out of what?

STEPHEN. Out of having for your sister-in-law a girl you thought tedious and unattractive. And still do. And still do.

SIMON. Look Stephen, this is really rather eccentric, even in the English fratricidal tradition. First you hold it against me that I won't join you in abusing yourself, and then you hold it against me that not only did I fail to abuse your intended wife eleven years ago, but won't join you in abusing her now that she is your wife and has borne you seven children—

STEPHEN. Six children.

SIMON. Nearly seven.

STEPHEN. Nearly six.

SIMON. Well, straight after the sixth, it'll be nearly seven. (*He gets up.*)

STEPHEN. Teresa's absolutely right about you. She always has been. You're just indifferent. Absolutely indifferent!

SIMON. In what sense? As a wine is indifferent, or prepositionally, as in, say, indifferent to—

STEPHEN. Imbeciles like Teresa. Go on, say it!

SIMON. But I don't want to say it.

STEPHEN. Not to me, no. But that's what you tell your clever-clever metropolitan Jeff Goldings, isn't it? That Teresa and I are imbeciles.

SIMON. I swear to you, Stephen, I've never told a soul.

STEPHEN. Answer me one question, Simon. *One* question! What have you got against having children?

SIMON. Well Steve, in the first place there isn't enough room. In the second place they seem to start by mucking up their parents' lives, and then go on in the third place to muck up their own. In the fourth place it doesn't seem right to bring them into a world like this in the fifth place and in the sixth place I don't like them very much in the first place. OK.

STEPHEN. And Beth? What about her?

SIMON (*after a little pause*). Beth and I have always known what we're doing, thank you Stephen.

STEPHEN. You think she's happy, do you?

SIMON. Yes, I do. And let's not let you say another word about her, because I don't want to hear it. Have you got that, Steve, *I don't want to hear it.* (*With low emphasis.*)

STEPHEN. No, I'm sure you don't. I'm sure you don't. The last thing you want to hear is how unhappy she is.

SIMON. Steve!

STEPHEN. Well, she is! So unhappy that last week she came around to Teresa and sobbed her heart out!

SIMON. Steve!

STEPHEN. She's having an affair, Simon. An affair with that Ned whom you so much despise. *That's* how unhappy your happy Beth is.

There is a long pause.

SIMON. With Ned. (*Pause.*) Beth's having an affair with Ned? (*Pause.*) Really? With Ned? Good God! (*Sits down.*)

STEPHEN. It's time you knew.

SIMON. No it isn't.

There is a pause.

STEPHEN. I had to tell you.

SIMON. Now that's a different matter.

There is the sound of a door opening left. BETH *enters.*

BETH. Hello. Hello, Stephen.

STEPHEN. Hello, Beth.

SIMON (*goes over, gives* BETH *a kiss*). You're back nice and early, aren't you?

BETH. Yes, I got an earlier train.

SIMON. Ah, that explains it. How was it, then, old Salisbury?

BETH. Old *Canterbury,* actually. Much as it ever was, except for the parts they've turned into new Canterbury.

SIMON. But the Cathedral's still there?

BETH. Although the French students were more interested in the new Marks and Spencers.

SIMON. And Ned?

BETH. Oh, he preferred the Cathedral.

STEPHEN. I really must be getting along. Headmaster will be wondering what's happening to me.

SIMON. Oh, but first you must tell Beth your news.

There is a slight pause.

The Assistant Headmastership, Steve.

STEPHEN. Oh. Oh yes. I got it.

BETH. Steve—how marvellous! (*Comes over, gives him a kiss.*) Congratulations—Teresa must be thrilled!

STEPHEN. Yes, she is. I've had some black moments since the interview, but she was absolutely sure—and old Si jollied me along a bit this morning. It's all a great relief, more than anything. Well, I really must dash—see you both very soon—(*goes towards the kitchen door*) Oh, by the way, Si—I was a bit carried away just now, spoke a lot of nonsense, don't know why I said it.

SIMON. Don't you?

STEPHEN. Yes, well I suppose I meant to hurt, but I didn't mean harm, if you see.

SIMON. Well then that's fine, because no harm's been done. I didn't take it seriously.

STEPHEN. Good. (*Hesitates, turns, goes out.*)

BETH. What did he say? (*Sits and lights a cigarette.*)

SIMON. Actually I could hardly make out—he was in a post-success depression, I think, suddenly realising that what he's got can therefore no longer be striven for. He'll be all right the moment he sets his sights on a full Headmastership. Or Amplesides is abolished. Triumph or disaster—you know, like a drug. What about tea or coffee?

BETH. No, I've had some, thanks.

SIMON. Where?

BETH. On the train.

SIMON. Oh, then you're probably still trying to work out which it was.

BETH. Did you enjoy your Wagner?

SIMON. I enjoyed some things about it, very much. The picture on its cover for example, its glossy and circular blackness when unsheathed, its light balance—and if the sound is any good it'll be quite perfect.

BETH. You haven't managed to play it then?

SIMON. Very nearly, very nearly. But what with Dave and Stephen, Jeff and Davina, the odd bod and sod, you know—

BETH. Oh, you poor thing, and you'd been looking forward to it all week.

SIMON. Still, one mustn't snatch at one's pleasures, nor overplan them it seems. (*He puts the record away in its box.*)

BETH (*pause*). How was Jeff?

SIMON. Oh, in excellent form, really. He got drunk, threw his scotch in his girl's face, dashed off to Cambridge where he's been having it off with his ex-wife, Gwynyth. Did you know Gwynyth, or was she a little before your time?

BETH. Isn't it Gwendoline?

SIMON. Yes, yes, Gwendoline. Anyway, usual sort of Jeff saga, quite droll in its way.

BETH. And what's his girl like?

SIMON. She's got good tits and a nasty sense of humour.

BETH. And did she try to get you to bed?

SIMON. She did.

BETH. And how did you get out of it?

SIMON. Rudely, I'm afraid as she's on to rather a good book, from the sound of it. Ah well—

BETH. Ah well, you can play your records now, can't you?

SIMON. Oh no. Wouldn't dream of it.

BETH. Why not?

SIMON. Well, for one thing, you hate Wagner.

BETH. Well, I'm going to have a bath.

SIMON. A four-hour bath?

BETH. Afterwards I've got to go along to the school—sort out the fares and docket them, that sort of thing.

SIMON. Ah! Well, in that case—

SIMON *moves to hi-fi and takes out record.* BETH *rises, hesitates, and moves towards him.*

BETH (*stops, looks at* SIMON). Stephen told you, didn't he?

SIMON. Mmmm? Told me what?

BETH. About me. At least I hope he has.

SIMON. Why?

BETH. So I shan't have to tell you myself.

SIMON. You don't have to.

BETH. What?

SIMON. Tell me.

BETH. What?

SIMON. Tell me anything you don't want to tell me. Stephen
said nothing of significance about anything.

BETH. But you see, I may not want to tell you, but I do want
you to know.

SIMON. Why?

BETH. Because there's an important problem we shall have to
discuss. And I want you to understand. (*Sits on sofa.*)

SIMON. In my experience, the worst thing you can do to an
important problem is discuss it. You know—(*sitting
down*)—I really do think this whole business of
non-communication is one of the more poignant fallacies of
our zestfully over-explanatory age. Most of us understand as
much as we need to without having to be told—except old
Dave, of course, now I thought he had quite an effective
system, a tribute really to the way in which even the lowest
amongst us can put our education (or lack of it, in Dave's
case) and intelligence (or lack of it, in Dave's case) to serving
our needs. He's done really remarkably well out of taking the
metaphors of courtesy literally, as for example when he asks
for a loan that is in fact a gift, and one replies, 'Of course,
Dave, no trouble, pay it back when you can.' *But* this system
completely collapses when he's faced with a plainly literal

reply, as for example when he asks to borrow our coffee set, and he's told that it'll be lent with reluctance and one would like him to be careful with it. Weird, isn't it, he can take one's courteous metaphors literally, but he can't take one's literals literally, he translates them into metaphors for insults, and plans, I'm reasonably happy to inform you, to move out at once. So I've managed one useful thing today, after all. When we come to think of his replacement, let's narrow our moral vision slightly, and settle for a pair of respectably married and out of date homosexuals who still think they've something to hide. They'll leave us entirely alone, and we can congratulate ourselves on doing them a good turn. We'll have to raise the rent to just this side of exorbitant of course, or they'll smell something fishy, but we'll pass the money straight on to charities for the aged, unmarried mothers, that sort of thing and no one need be the wiser, what do you think?

BETH. In other words, you do know.

SIMON. In other words, can't we confine ourselves to the other words.

BETH. What did Stephen tell you, please Simon.

SIMON. Nothing. Nothing, except for the odd detail, that I haven't known for a long time. So you see it's all right. Nothing's changed for the worst, though it might if we assume we have to talk about it.

BETH (*long pause*). How long have you known for?

SIMON. Oh—(*sighs*) about ten months it would be roughly. (*Pause.*) How long has it been going on for?

BETH. For about ten months, it would be. (*Pause.*) How did you know?

SIMON. There's no point, Beth—

BETH. Yes, there is. Yes, there is. How did you know?

SIMON. Well, frankly, your sudden habit, after years of
admirable conversational economy on such day-to-day
matters as what you'd done today, of becoming a trifle prolix.

BETH. You mean you knew I was having an affair because I
became boring?

SIMON. No, no, over-detailed, that's all, darling. And quite
naturally, as you were anxious to account for stretches of time
in which you assumed I *would* be interested if I knew how
you'd *actually* filled them, if you see, so you sweetly devoted
considerable effort and paradoxically imaginative skill to
rendering them—for my sake I know—totally uninteresting.
My eyes may have been glazed but my heart was touched.

BETH. Thank you. And is that all you had to go on?

SIMON. Well, you have doubled your bath routine. Time was,
you took one immediately before going out for the day. These
last ten months you've taken one immediately on return too.
(*Pause.*) And once or twice you've addressed me, when in the
twilight zone, with an unfamiliar endearment.

BETH. What was it?

SIMON. Foxy. (*Little pause.*) At least, I took it to be an
endearment. Is it?

BETH. Yes. I'm sorry.

SIMON. No, no, it's quite all right.

BETH. You haven't felt it's interfered with your sex-life then?

SIMON. On the contrary. *Quite* the contrary. In fact there
seems to have been an increased intensity in your—(*gestures*)
which I suppose in itself was something of a sign.

BETH. In what way?

SIMON. Well, guilt, would it be? A desire to make up—

BETH (*after a pause*). And did you know it was Ned, too?

SIMON. Ned *too?* Oh, did I also know it was Ned? No, that was
the little detail I mentioned Stephen did provide. Ned. There I
was surprised.

BETH. Why?

SIMON. Oh, I don't know. Perhaps because—well, no offence
to Ned, whom I've *always* as you know thought of as a very
engaging chap, in his way, no offence to *you* either, come to
think of it, I'd just imagined when you did have an affair it
would be with someone of more—more—

BETH. What?

SIMON. Consequence. *Overt* consequence.

BETH. He's of consequence to me.

SIMON. And *that's* what matters, quite.

BETH. What did you mean, when?

SIMON. Mmmm?

BETH. *When* I had an affair, you said.

SIMON. A grammatical slip, that's all. And since the hypothesis
is now a fact—

BETH. But you used the emphatic form—when I *did* have an
affair—which implies that you positively assumed I'd have an
affair. Didn't you?

SIMON. Well, given your nature, darling, and the fact that so
many people do have them these days, I can't see any reason
for being bouleversé now that you're having one, even with
Ned, can I put it that way?

BETH. Given what about my nature?

SIMON. It's marvellously responsive—warm, a warm,
responsive nature. And then I realized once we'd taken the
decision not to have children,—and the fact that you work

every day and therefore meet chaps—and pretty exotic ones
too, from lithe young Spanish counts to experienced Japanese
businessmen—not forgetting old Ned himself—it was only
realistic—

BETH. From boredom, you mean. You know I'm having an
affair because I'm boring, and you assumed I'd have one from
boredom. That's why I'm in love with Ned, is it?

SIMON. I'm absolutely prepared to think of Ned as a very,
very lovable fellow. I'm sure *his* wife loves him, why shouldn't
mine.

BETH. You are being astonishingly hurtful.

SIMON. I don't want to be, I don't want to be! That's why I
tried to avoid this conversation, darling.

BETH. You'd like to go back, would you, to where I came in,
and pretend that I'd simply caught the early train from
Salisbury, and here I was, old unfaithful Beth, back home and
about to take her bath, as usual?

SIMON. Yes, I'd love to. (*Little pause.*) I thought it was
Canterbury.

BETH. It was neither. We spent the night in a hotel in Euston,
and the morning in Ned's poky little office at the school,
agonizing.

SIMON. Agonizing? Good God, did you really?

BETH. About whether we should give up everything to live
together properly.

SIMON. Properly?

BETH. We want, you see, to be husband and wife to each other.

SIMON. Husband *and* wife to each other? Is Ned up to such
double duty? And what did you decide?

BETH. Do you care?

SIMON. Yes.

BETH. His wife isn't well. She's been under psychiatric treatment for years. And his daughter is autistic.

SIMON. Oh. I'm sorry. I can quite see why he wants to leave them.

BETH. But I could still leave you.

SIMON. Yes.

BETH. But you don't think I will. Do you?

SIMON. No.

BETH. And why not?

SIMON. Because I hope you'd rather live with me than anybody else, except Ned of course. And I know you'd rather live with almost anyone than live alone.

BETH. You think I am that pathetic?

SIMON. I don't think it's pathetic. I'd rather live with you than anyone else, including Ned. And I don't want to live alone either.

BETH. But do you want to live at all?

SIMON. What?

BETH. As you hold such a deeply contemptuous view of human life. That's Ned's diagnosis of you.

SIMON. But the description of my symptoms came from you, did it?

BETH. He says you're one of those men who only give permission to little bits of life to get through to you. He says that while we may envy you your serenity, we should be revolted by the rot from which it stems. Your sanity is of the kind that causes people to go quietly mad around you.

SIMON. What an elegant paraphrase. Tell me, did you take notes?

BETH. I didn't have to. Every word rang true.

SIMON. But if it's all true, why do you need to keep referring it back to Ned?

BETH. It's a way of keeping in touch with him. If I forgot in the middle of a sentence that he's there and mine, I might begin to scream at you and claw at you and punch at you.

SIMON. But why should you want to do that?

BETH. Because I hate you.

The telephone rings. SIMON *makes a move towards it. After the fourth ring, it stops.*

SIMON. Oh, of course. I've put on the machine. (*Pause.*)

BETH (*quietly*). You know the most insulting thing, that you let me go on and on being unfaithful without altering your manner or your behaviour one—one—you don't care about me, or my being in love with somebody else, or my betraying you, good God! least of all that! But you do wish I hadn't actually *mentioned* it, because then we could have gone on, at least *you* could, pretending that everything was all right, no, not even pretending, as far as *you* were concerned, everything was all right, you probably still think it *is* all right—and—and—you've—you've—all those times we've made love, sometimes the very same evening as Ned and I—and yet you took me—in your usual considerate fashion, just as you take your third of a bottle of wine with dinner or your carefully measured brandy and your cigar after it, *and* enjoyed it all the more because I felt guilty, God help me *guilty* and so tried harder for your sake—and you *admit* that, no, not admit it, simply state it as if on the difference made by an extra voice or something in your bloody Wagner —don't you see, don't you see that that makes you a freak! You're—you're—Oh, damn! Damn. Damn you. (*Pause.*) Oh, damn.

There is a silence.

So you might as well listen to your Wagner.

SIMON. I must say you've quite warmed up for it. And what are *you* going to do, have your cleansing bath?

BETH. No, go to Ned for a couple of hours.

SIMON. Oh dear, more agonizing in his poky little office. Or is that a euphemism for Ned's brand of love-play? Excuse me, but what precisely has all this been about? You complain of my reticence over the last ten months, but what good has all this exposition served, what's it been for Beth? Ned's not going to leave his wife, I don't want you to leave me, you don't even think you're going to leave me—we have a perfectly sensible arrangement, we are happy enough together you and I, insultingly so if you like but still happy. We could go on and on, with Ned, until you've gone off him, why, why did you have to muck it up between you with your infantile agonizings.

BETH. Because there's a problem.

SIMON. What problem?

BETH. I'm going to have a baby.

SIMON (*stares at her for a long moment*). What? (*Another moment.*) Whose?

BETH. *That* is the problem. (*Goes out.*)

SIMON *sits in a state of shock.* DAVE *enters left.*

DAVE (*stands grinning at* SIMON). Well, I worked it out, you'll be unhappy to hear. Suzy put me onto you. She just

laughed when I told her the stuff you'd said, she and her bloke
had dealings with your type in their last place. You were
trying to get me out, that's all. Well, it hasn't worked, see. I'm
staying. See. And another thing, Suzy and her bloke are
looking for a new place. I said they could move in upstairs
with me. Got that? Got that? You won't like tangling with
them either. (*Stares at* SIMON.) Having a bit of trouble
sinking in, is it? (*Turns, goes out, leaving the door open.*)

SIMON *remains sitting, dazed. Then he goes to the drinks
table, pours himself a small scotch. Looks at it. Frowns. Adds
some more. Stands uncertainly, looks at the telephone, goes
over to it. Remembers something vaguely, presses the
play-back machine.*

WOOD (*his voice*). Hello, Hench, Bernard Wood, né Strapley
here. I expect by now my little visit has passed entirely out of
your consciousness, it was all of an hour ago that I left, and
you've no doubt had any number of amusing little things to
engage your attention. Your life goes on its self-appointed
way, as I sit in my empty flat, my home. I've taken off my
jacket, and I've lowered my braces so that they dangle around
me—a picture, you might say, of old Wood, né Strapley, quite
abandoned at the last. Imagine it, the jacket off, the braces
down, thinking of you as I speak into the telephone, clasped
tightly in my left hand as my right brings up, not trembling
too much—Hench—sweet little Hench—and point the gun at
my forehead—no, through the—no, I can't do the mouth, the
metal tastes too intimate—it'll have to be—picture it—picture
it—and as I—as I—Hench, as I squeeze—squee . . .

SIMON *switches off the machine, interrupting the message.
He sits motionless.*
JEFF *appears in the doorway left.*

SIMON (*sees him. Gets up slowly*). Ah yes. Jeff. Yes. All right,
are we then? Get back to—(*thinks*) Oxford, did you?

JEFF. I didn't get to the bloody corner.

SIMON. Oh really. Why not?

JEFF. There was a police car, Simon, right behind me, then right beside me, then right on bloody top of me with the cops all bloody over me, breathalysing me, shaking me about, and then down at the station for the rest of it. That's why bloody not. And you tipped the buggers off, friend, Christ!

SIMON. What? (*Vaguely.*) What?

JEFF. No, don't deny it, don't deny it, please Christ don't deny it. Davina told me when I phoned her. She told me—you tipped them off. Christ!

SIMON. Oh. (*Thinks.*) That's what you believe, is it?

JEFF. That's what I bloody know, Simon.

SIMON (*calmly*). What sort of man do you think I am? (*He throws his scotch in* JEFF's *face.*) What sort of man do you think I am?

JEFF (*sputtering, gasping*). Christ, Christ! My eyes! My eyes!

SIMON *watches him a moment, then takes out his handkerchief, gives it to* JEFF.

Christ—(*Takes the handkerchief.*) Thanks. (*Little pause.*) Thanks. (*Little pause.*) Sorry. Sorry, Simon. (*Pause, goes and sits down.*) Can I have a drink? (*Pause.*) The bitch.

SIMON *hesitates, then goes and gets him a scotch, brings it to him.*

Thanks.

There is a pause.

Don't throw me out, eh? I've got nowhere to bloody go, and I don't want to go there yet.

SIMON. I'm going to play Parsifal. Do you mind?

JEFF. No, lovely. Lovely.

SIMON. You sure?

JEFF. Christ yes. You know I adore Wagner.

SIMON. No, I didn't know that.

JEFF. Christ, I introduced you. At Oxford. I bloody introduced you.

SIMON. Did you really? (*Looks at him.*) Such a long time ago. Then I owe you more than I can say. Thank you, Jeff. (*Goes over to the hi-fi, puts on the record.*)

The opening bars of Parsifal *fill the theatre. They sit listening as the music swells.*
The light fades.

Curtain.